STONE CIRCLES

Discover Stone, Bronze and Iron Age Britain

Written by John Malam

WAYLAND

CONTENTS

STONE, BRONZE AND IRON

Christian Thomsen had a problem to solve. It was the year 1816 and he was putting on a display at a museum in Copenhagen, the capital of Denmark.
  Thomsen had hundreds of prehistoric objects for the display, but he didn't know how old any of them were. He decided to put them into order, from the oldest to the youngest. He divided the objects into three groups, based on what they were made of. He decided the oldest objects were made of stone. Then came metal objects made from bronze. In the last group he put metal objects made of iron. Thomsen had invented the **Three Age System**.

The Three Age System in Britain

Stone Age
(800,000 years ago to 2300BCE)
Tools, weapons and other objects were
made from pieces of stone, especially flint.

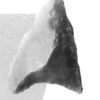

Flint
arrowhead

Bronze Age
(2300BCE to 800BCE)
Stone was replaced by metal. Copper was the first metal used.
Then came a harder metal called bronze.

Bronze
axe

Iron Age
(800BCE to 43CE)
Bronze gave way to iron, an even harder metal.
The Iron Age ended in 43CE, when the Romans invaded Britain.

Iron
spearhead

The Stone Age is divided into three periods:

1. Old Stone Age
or the Palaeolithic
800,000 to 10,000 years ago
Much of this period is called
the Ice Age, because sheets of
ice covered most of the land.

2. Middle Stone Age
or the Mesolithic
10,000 years ago to 4000BCE
The ice melted and groups of
hunter-gatherer people moved
across Britain.

3. New Stone Age
or the Neolithic
4000BCE to 2300BCE
The time of the first farmers
and villages in Britain.

BEFORE HISTORY

There have been humans in Britain for about 800,000 years. That is an incredibly long time in our human story. For nearly all of this time, our ancestors lived in a period we call 'prehistory'.

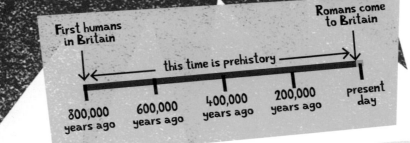

First humans in Britain

this time is prehistory

Romans come to Britain

800,000 years ago | 600,000 years ago | 400,000 years ago | 200,000 years ago | present day

The time before history

Prehistory is the time before people started to write things down. The Romans brought writing to Britain when they came here about 2,000 years ago. From that point, events were recorded in writing and are known as 'history'. Everything that happened before the Romans was a time before history began – it was prehistory.

The word 'pre' means 'before'. So, the word 'prehistory' means 'before history'.

Prehistory detectives

For hundreds of years, people have found things buried in the ground that don't seem to belong there. Pottery, beads, bones and even buildings all belonging to early people and civilisations have been buried over time. People who look for and study these ancient objects are called archaeologists.

Uncovering a Neolithic ceremonial site on the island of Mainland, Orkney, Scotland.

BRITAIN'S PREHISTORIC PLACES

There are thousands of prehistoric places in Britain, and more are being discovered all the time. This map shows where some of Britain's stone and timber circles are to be found. You'll find out about some of them in this book.

RING OF BRODGAR

CALLANISH

Grey Wethers

LONG MEG

CASTLERIGG

ARBOR LOW

SEAHENGE

ROLLRIGHT STONES

AVEBURY

WOODHENGE

GREY WETHERS

STONEHENGE

Winter at Woodhenge

STONE CIRCLES

Thousands of years ago, prehistoric people moved massive stones across the land, then stood them up into circles. The people are long gone, but the stone circles they made are still there for us to see today.

What are stone circles?

Stone circles are rings of stones standing upright in the ground. Each circle is different: the smallest circles are only about 4m across, and the largest are more than 100m across. The stones can be tall or short, there are spaces between them, and sometimes there is a ditch around the circle.

Today, there are about 1,000 stone circles in Britain and Ireland. No one knows how many circles were ever built, but it was probably many more than this.

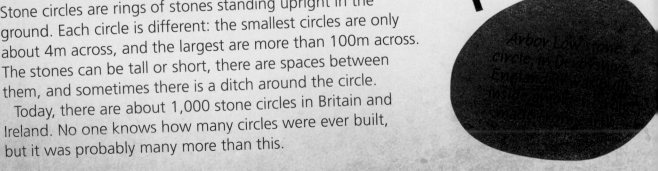

Arbor Low stone circle in Derbyshire, England, is so old that its stones have all fallen over.

'Seahenge' timber circle

'Seahenge'

In one very rare case, a complete timber circle, made from 55 upright wooden posts, has been found on a beach in Norfolk, eastern England. The circle is known as 'Seahenge'. Archaeologists looked at the 'tree rings' in the posts. These are growth rings of varying width made each year a tree is alive. From the pattern of tree rings the archaeologists discovered that the trees had all been cut down in the year 2049BCE. This proved the circle had been built in the Bronze Age, about 4,000 years ago.

As the sea level rose, the timber circle was covered by water. The seawater stopped the wood rotting away.

When and where

The first stone circles were built around 3300BCE, in the Neolithic period. The last ones were put up in the Bronze Age, about 1500BCE. This means that prehistoric people were building stone circles for about 1,800 years.

Most stone circles were built in hilly, upland areas, where suitable stone was to be found. In some places, such as the Lake District in England and Aberdeenshire in Scotland, there are several circles quite close together.

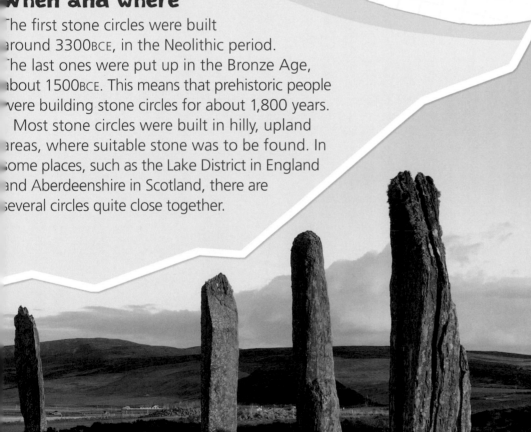

WHY WERE STONE CIRCLES BUILT?

Prehistoric people must have built stone circles for a purpose. The circles were important to them, but why? As they went out of use, people eventually forgot what the circles were for and they became a prehistoric mystery.

Old ideas

About a thousand years ago, people thought that stone circles had been built by giants. It was their way of explaining them. Later on, people said they were temples where sacrifices were made.

New ideas

Here are some of the ideas people have today about why stone circles were built.

• Places to remember the dead

The bones of ancient people have been found at stone circles. Perhaps they were leaders and other important people. Archaeologists think this might mean stone circles were places where people came to remember the dead.

Stonehenge is the most famous stone circle of them all. Archaeologists are still discovering its secrets.

Stone knights

A strange myth surrounds the Rollright Stones, in Oxfordshire. Stories tell of a great king and his knights who set out to conquer all of England. A witch put a stop to their ambitions by turning them to stone. Some say though, that they will one day rise again and continue their quest!

The tallest of the Rollright Stones.

• Meeting places
Archaeologists think people may have gathered at stone circles on special occasions.

• Healing places
Archaeologists wonder if sick and injured people went to stone circles in the belief the stones had magical powers to heal them.

• To mark the changing seasons
Some stone circles were used to keep track of time, like giant clocks. They marked the movement of the sun or the moon through the year. This helped prehistoric people know when the seasons began and ended.

UNIQUE STONEHENGE

In south-west England, in the county of Wiltshire, are the ruins of Stonehenge. It is the most famous stone circle in Britain, and there is nothing like it anywhere else in the world.

What's so special about Stonehenge?

For a start, it isn't just one circle but two circles, one inside the other. The outer circle is made of tall stones with flat stones, called lintels, sitting on top of them. Only Stonehenge has lintel stones.

What's more, the inner circle is made from short stones called bluestones. These were brought to Stonehenge from south Wales, a distance of about 240km. No other stone circle uses stones from far away.

Stonehenge as it is today. Over the years, some stones have fallen down.

The Stonehenge jigsaw

For archaeologists, Stonehenge is like a prehistoric jigsaw. There are many pieces, and the challenge is working out how they all once fitted together.

Sarsen trilithons: the tallest sarsen stones, standing inside the stone circle in the shape of a horseshoe. Each trilithon has two upright stones and one lintel stone. 'Tri' means 'three' and 'lithon' means 'stones'.

The Heel Stone: marks the position of the sun as it rises above Stonehenge on Midsummer's Day.

Bluestone stone circle: the inner stone circle, made from short, upright stones. They're called bluestones because they look blue-green when wet.

Circular earthwork: two wide, circular banks of earth, and a ditch.

The Avenue: a long path from the River Avon to Stonehenge.

Why it's called Stonehenge
No one knows what prehistoric people called Stonehenge. It got its name about 1,000 years ago, when Anglo-Saxon people called it 'Stanenges'. It meant 'hanging' or 'hinging stones', after the lintel stones across the top of the upright stones. Over the years, the spelling changed until it became 'Stonehenge'.

Aubrey Holes: a circle of about 56 pits just inside the bank of earth (named after John Aubrey, who discovered them).

Sarsen stone circle: the outer stone circle of tall, upright stones with lintel stones. It's made from sarsen sandstone. It might never have been finished.

This artwork shows what Stonehenge might have looked like at the height of its use.

AROUND STONEHENGE

Stonehenge might seem to stand alone on a grassy plain. But if you look at the wider area, you can see it has always been part of a busy landscape.

A waterway

Flowing through the Stonehenge landscape is the River Avon. It must have been important to prehistoric people, because they built several places close to it. When Stonehenge was being built, the river was probably used to transport the bluestones to the building site.

Route to Stonehenge

A long path, called the Avenue, joins the River Avon to Stonehenge. It is about 2.5km long. Some archaeologists think this was a special route, along which prehistoric people travelled to Stonehenge.

▲ BARROWS

DURRINGTON WALLS

WOODHENGE

THE AVENUE

STONEHENGE

RIVER AVON

Humps and bumps

In the fields around Stonehenge are lots of small, grassy mounds. Some are on their own, others are in groups. These are Bronze Age barrows where people carried out religious ceremonies and buried their dead - inside are the remains of prehistoric people. Many powerful people chose to bury their dead close to Stonehenge, showing that the circle continued to be important hundreds of years after it was built.

A group of Bronze Age round barrows close to Stonehenge.

Durrington Walls

About 3km north-east of Stonehenge is Durrington Walls. It's a 'henge': a deep circular ditch, with breaks in it for people to walk across. The soil from digging out the ditch was piled up to make a bank on the outside of the ditch. The Durrington Walls henge is 470m in diameter, and standing inside it were two circles of wooden posts.

Woodhenge

Close to Durrington Walls is 'Woodhenge'. It was built at the same time as Stonehenge, but out of wood. Woodhenge was six circles made from wooden posts built one inside the other.

The circles at Woodhenge are marked out today by concrete posts.

GRAND DESIGNS

Stonehenge started off as something quite small, and was then rebuilt several times. It took about 800 years before it became the Stonehenge we see today.

c.3000BCE
– the first Stonehenge

The first Stonehenge was not a stone circle at all. It was a deep ditch with banks of earth surrounding a wide, circular space. There were two entrances into the space and around the edge was a ring of 56 deep pits (the Aubrey Holes) that may have held stones or wooden posts.

c.2500BCE
– the second Stonehenge

After about 500 years, Stonehenge was completely rebuilt. Large and small stones were brought from near and far. The massive sarsen stones were put up in a circle about 30m across. Lintel stones were placed across their tops.

Stones were put up inside the new circle. Tall trilithons were set in a horseshoe shape and short bluestones were arranged in two horseshoes, one inside the other.

Carvings on the stones

If you look closely at certain Stonehenge stones you'll see carvings. You might recognise axes and daggers: these were carved by Bronze Age people in about 1500BCE. There are many more carvings that are no longer visible to the naked eye!

Axes carved on the Stonehenge stones in the Bronze Age, about 1500BCE.

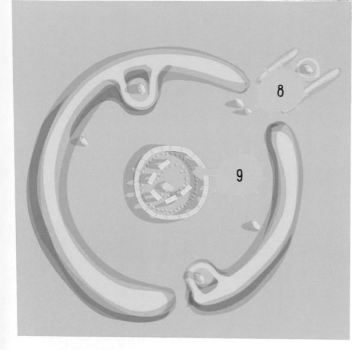

c.2200BCE
– the third Stonehenge

After about 300 years, the bluestones were moved to new positions inside the sarsen stone circle. When the work was finished, most of the bluestones formed a circle of their own. Stonehenge then had two stone circles – the outer sarsen circle and the inner bluestone circle. The ruins we see today are of this final version of Stonehenge.

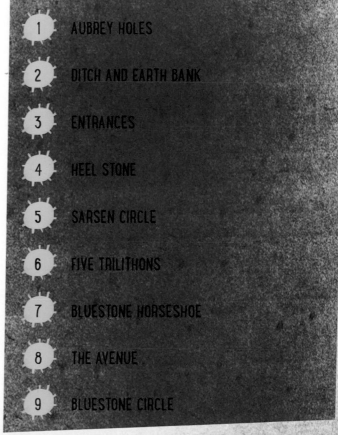

1. AUBREY HOLES
2. DITCH AND EARTH BANK
3. ENTRANCES
4. HEEL STONE
5. SARSEN CIRCLE
6. FIVE TRILITHONS
7. BLUESTONE HORSESHOE
8. THE AVENUE
9. BLUESTONE CIRCLE

MOVING WITH MANPOWER!

It was a huge effort to build Stonehenge. The stones had to be found and then they had to be moved to the site – imagine the back-breaking work to do that!

The gap between the upright stones is less than 1.5m.

Short distance sarsen stones

The tallest and heaviest stones are made from sarsen sandstone. They came from as far away as the Marlborough Downs, about 30km north of Stonehenge. The upright stones weigh between 25 and 35 tonnes each, and the lintel stones are about 7 tonnes each.

Archaeologists have worked out that it would have taken about 200 people 12 days to drag each of the 40 upright stones to the building site. They think the stones were put on wooden sledges that people pulled along using ropes.

When it was finished, Stonehenge probably had about 75 sarsen stones – 40 uprights and 35 lintels across the tops of the stones.

PRESELI HILLS

BRISTOL CHANNEL

MARLBOROUGH DOWNS

STONEHENGE

Long distance bluestones

The shorter and lighter stones are made from bluestone. Bluestone is not found near Stonehenge. Instead, the builders brought the bluestones from the Preseli Hills of south Wales, about 240km away.

Archaeologists think the bluestones were brought to Stonehenge by boat. They could have travelled around the coast of south Wales, and then inland along rivers. Finally, they were dragged a short distance overland to Stonehenge.

Rough to smooth

Archaeologists have found small strong stones that they believe were used as hammers. The standing stones were quite rough when they arrived at the building site. The builders wanted them to have smooth sides, so they bashed away at the rough stones with the hammerstones, chipping pieces off until they were smooth. Archaeologists have found lots of chippings too!

Marks left by hammerstones to smooth the rough surface.

RAISING THE STONES

Once the heavy stones were at the building site, the hard work of standing them up could begin. But, before the stones could go up, the builders had to dig down.

Going up

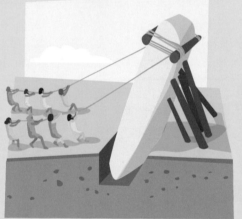

Each stone stands in a deep pit called a stone hole. The builders tied ropes to each stone and dragged it to the edge of its stone hole until it toppled in.

Once it was in the hole, there was a lot more pulling to be done until the stone was standing straight up.

The hole was then packed with soil and rocks to keep the stone in place.

Lintel stones

To get the lintels on top of the standing stones, the builders might have used wooden platforms. The platforms went up one layer at a time, slowly raising the lintels until they were at the right height to be placed on top of the standing stones.

The bumps and hollows had to line up, or the lintels would not fit.

Joining the stones

The tops of the standing stones are not flat. Instead, the builders shaped the tops. Each standing stone has a round 'bump' of stone on the top. The lintel stones have two hollows in them — one at each end.

When the lintels were raised onto the standing stones, the hollows and bumps slotted into place, locking the stones together.

Who were the builders?

In 2004, archaeologists were digging at Durrington Walls (3km from Stonehenge) when they found the remains of houses — it was the first Neolithic village ever found in southern Britain.

People lived in the Durrington Walls village in about 2500BCE. This was the same time as the big stones at Stonehenge were being put into place. Because of this, archaeologists wonder if the Stonehenge builders lived in the village.

A fallen lintel stone with its hollow. It once sat on top of the tall stone behind it.

WHY WAS STONEHENGE BUILT?

Prehistoric people worked hard to build Stonehenge and used it for about 2,000 years. But what was Stonehenge for? What did people do there?

Prehistoric sun temple

There are no remains of houses at Stonehenge, so it was not a place where people lived. It was not built with solid walls (like a castle), so Stonehenge was not a place to shelter in times of trouble. Just what was the purpose of Stonehenge?

Archaeologists think it was a prehistoric sun temple, where people gathered at special times of the year.

The most important day of the year

The builders of Stonehenge carefully placed the stones to be in line with the sun on two days of the year:

- Midsummer's Day, 21st June – the longest day of the year, also called the summer solstice

- Midwinter's Day, 21st December – the shortest day of the year, also called the winter solstice

It's thought that Midwinter's Day was the most important day. Prehistoric people were farmers. For them, it marked the start of the new year when the dark, cold days of winter gave way to the lighter, warmer days of spring. This was the start of the new growing season, when they could begin to plant fresh crops to feed them for the year ahead.

A place of healing?

Another clue to why Stonehenge was built might lie in the mysterious bluestones. Archaeologists question why they were brought 240km from Wales. Folk tales from Wales say these stones have healing powers, so did sick and injured people go to Stonehenge to be healed by the power of the bluestones?

In line with the sun

At dawn on Midsummer's Day the sun rises behind the Heel Stone and rays of sunlight shine into the centre of Stonehenge.

Exactly six months later, on Midwinter's Day, the setting sun drops down in line with the stones of the largest trilithon. As the sun's light fades, Stonehenge is left in darkness.

The shorter bluestones are inside the outer sarsen circle.

The sun rises at Stonehenge on Midsummer's Day at about 4:45am.

LONG MEG AND HER DAUGHTERS

In the county of Cumbria, in the north-west of England, a strange tale is told about the stone circle known as Long Meg and her Daughters...

One day, a witch was watching as her many daughters danced in a circle. But then a wizard appeared and cast a spell that turned them all to stone!

Squashed circle

This stone circle was built about 4,500 years ago. It's not a perfect circle, but is very slightly 'squashed', like an oval. At its widest, the circle is about 110m across.

Today there are 59 stones in the circle, but when it was built there might have been as many as 70. Over the centuries, some stones have been dug up and taken away by local farmers to use as building stones. Some of the stones are massive – the heaviest one weighs about 30 tonnes. It would have taken more than 100 people to pull it into a standing position.

The stone known as Long Meg is outside the circle.

Long Meg

Just outside the entrance to the circle is a tall stone standing on its own. This is Long Meg – it's twice as tall as an adult.

The prehistoric people who built the circle chose a special place to put Long Meg. As they stood in the centre of the circle on Midwinter's Day they would have seen the sun set in line with Long Meg, signalling the start of the new year.

Rock art

The Long Meg standing stone has mysterious carvings on it made by prehistoric people. There's a spiral pattern, circles and some small holes, all carved into the surface. This prehistoric rock art shows that Long Meg must have been an important stone. To this day, no one knows what the carvings mean.

CALLANISH

In the far north of Britain is the island of Lewis. It's in the Atlantic Ocean, off the west coast of Scotland. Prehistoric people arrived there about 5,000 years ago, and soon afterwards they built Callanish – now known as the Stonehenge of the North.

A myth says the stones were giants who were turned to stone for refusing to convert to Christianity.

Small circle

The rocky island of Lewis provided all the material that was needed for the circle. Prehistoric people split the island's stone into flat slabs, which they used to create a small circle of 13 tall, thin stones. In the centre they placed the largest stone. It towers above the rest at 4.75m tall.

Rows of stones

Leading up to the central circle are five long rows of standing stones. Two of the rows are side by side, marking out an avenue that people probably walked along as they made their way to the circle.

Achaeologists believe there were going to be four avenues of standing stones leading to the circle, but only one avenue was completed.

It's hard to imagine the stones were once buried under peat.

Hidden under peat

Callanish was built in the Neolithic period, about 4,500 years ago. Over the years, a deep layer of peat built up around the standing stones until only the tops could be seen. It was only when the peat was dug away that the full height of the stones was revealed.

More prehistoric sites

Like Stonehenge, Callanish was part of an important prehistoric landscape. After the main stone circle was constructed, a later generation added a tomb in the very centre. There are other stone circles nearby, as well as single standing stones, an ancient settlement and a timber circle.

From the air, you can more easily see the Callanish stone circle and the rows of stones.

THREE IN ONE

The Great Circle at Avebury is the largest stone circle in Britain. It's so wide that a village stands inside it and cars drive through it. And when you look closer, you see two smaller stone circles are also inside it!

Building Avebury

Like Stonehenge, the Avebury stone circles stand in south-west England, in the county of Wiltshire. The Great Circle is about 400m across. It was built from 98 sarsen stones. This is the same type of rock used to build the outer circle at Stonehenge.
Inside the Great Circle are two more stone circles, both about 90m across.

The huge size of Avebury can only really be seen from the air – the houses give an idea of how big it is!

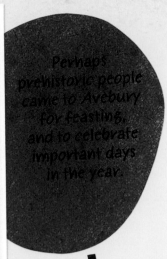

Perhaps prehistoric people came to Avebury for feasting, and to celebrate important days in the year.

Deep ditch

As well as the stone circles, prehistoric people also made a massive earthwork at Avebury. It was a deep ditch and a high bank of soil that went all the way around the Great Circle. The ditch was about 9m deep! There were four places to cross the ditch, which is how people reached the stone circles.

The stones at Avebury are all sizes and shapes.

Crushed to death

In the 1300s, people thought Avebury was a pagan (non-Christian) place. They tried to destroy it by pushing some of the stones over and burying them. A man was killed when a massive stone fell on him. His skeleton was found by archaeologists in 1938.

Avebury avenues

Avebury is also famous for its rows, or avenues, of standing stones. There were two avenues of stones, each one about 1.6km long. Because they go all the way to the circles, it's thought prehistoric people walked along them. They crossed over the ditch and were then inside the Great Circle.

STONE CIRCLES TODAY

The last stone circles were built about 4,000 years ago. No one knows why prehistoric people stopped building them, so today, we want to find out as much about them as we can.

Archaeologists have used concrete blocks at some circles to mark where stones and timber posts once stood. This is the Sanctuary, near Avebury.

Why were stone circles abandoned?

After generations of use, stone circles fell out of use. Perhaps people's ideas and traditions changed and they were no longer thought important. Or, perhaps prehistoric people's lives changed and not enough manpower could be called on to build them.

Britain's stone circles are protected by law. It is illegal to damage them in any way.

Stone circle detectives

Stone circles are studied by archaeologists, who have many different ways to find out about them. They photograph them and make careful maps showing where all the stones are. Lasers scan the stones looking for signs of prehistoric art.

Searching for clues

Archaeologists also dig into the ground, looking for clues that will help them find out about stone circles. Here are some of the things that archaeologists find:

★ Pieces of prehistoric pottery, stone tools, animal and human bones;

★ Holes where stones and wooden posts once stood;

★ Seeds and tiny grains of pollen from plants that used to grow near the stone circles.

The Amesbury Archer

In 2002, a new primary school was being built at Amesbury, about 5km from Stonehenge. Archaeologists were called in to examine the building site, and what they found made headlines around the world.

Buried in the ground was the skeleton of a man. He'd been buried with flint arrowheads and two wristguards, so archaeologists think he must have been an archer. He was given the name the 'Amesbury Archer'. His bones revealed that he was a traveller who had come all the way from the south of Europe, and had been buried at the time of Stonehenge.

In honour of this ancient visitor, the primary school was called Amesbury Archer Primary School.

Stonehenge is so famous that in 1929 a concrete replica of it was built at Maryhill, Washington, USA.

The Amesbury Archer might have come specially to visit Stonehenge.

STONEHENGE IN NUMBERS

2.5km long, the Stonehenge Avenue

30 lintel stones originally across the sarsen uprights

118 Bronze Age axes and daggers carved on the sarsen stones

7.3m high, the tallest sarsen stone (in a trilithon)

200 people to drag each sarsen stone

3 trilithons still standing today

30 upright sarsen stones originally in the outer stone circle

75 sarsen stones originally in the whole of Stonehenge

30km, the distance to bring the sarsens

56 Aubrey Holes (might be pits where stones or posts once stood)

1 million visitors to Stonehenge every year

5 trilithons originally set in a horseshoe shape

60 bluestones originally in the inner stone circle

12 days to drag each sarsen stone to the site

17 upright sarsen stones still standing today

30m diameter, the outer sarsen circle

7 tonnes in weight, each lintel stone

4 tonnes in weight, each bluestone

240km, the distance to bring the bluestones from south Wales

35 tonnes in weight, the heaviest sarsen stone (in a trilithon)

GLOSSARY

archaeologist (say: are-kee-ol-o-ist) A person who finds out about the past, usually by digging things up.

avenue A long path, sometimes with standing stones on either side, leading towards a stone circle.

bluestone A type of hard stone with a slightly blue colour.

bronze A metal made by mixing copper and tin. It's harder than copper, but softer than iron.

earthwork A structure in which earth (soil) is the main building component. Banks and ditches are earthworks.

flint A type of stone that was chipped into shape to make tools such as axes, arrowheads and scrapers.

hammerstone A heavy stone used as a hammer.

henge A type of prehistoric place made in the Neolithic period. It was a circular enclosure surrounded by a ditch and a bank of earth.

lintel stone A stone block across the tops of pairs of standing stones.

Mesolithic (say: mez-o-lith-ik) The Middle Stone Age period, about 10,000 years ago to 4000BC.

Neolithic (say: nee-o-lith-ik) The New Stone Age period, about 4000BC to 2300BC.

Palaeolithic (say: pal-e-o-lith-ik) The Old Stone Age period, about 800,000 to 10,000 years ago.

peat A type of wet, spongy, brown material grown from rotting plants.

prehistory The time in human history before writing began.

rock art Patterns carved into rock by prehistoric people.

sarsen A type of hard sandstone used to build prehistoric places, such as the stone circles at Avebury and Stonehenge.

standing stone A stone made to stand upright in the ground.

stone hole A hole dug into the ground for a standing stone to fit into.

Three Age System A way of dividing prehistory into three parts - Stone Age, Bronze Age and Iron Age.

trilithon Two upright stones with a third stone, a lintel stone, across the top. It means "three stones".

wristguard Protection worn by archers on their wrists.

Understanding dates

• The letters 'BCE' stand for 'Before Common Era'.

• The letters 'CE' stand for 'Common Era'.

• BCE dates are counted backwards from the year 1. CE dates are counted forwards from the year 1. There was no year 0.

• Some dates have a 'c.' in front of them. This stands for 'circa' (say: sur-ca), which means 'about'. These dates are guesses, because no one knows exactly what the real date is.

INDEX

First published in Great Britain in 2016 by Wayland
Copyright © Wayland, 2016

All rights reserved.

Author: John Malam
Consultant: Mark Bowden, Historic England
Editor: Annabel Stones

Historic England is a Government service championing England's heritage and giving expert, constructive advice.

ISBN: 9781526301598
10 9 8 7 6 5 4 3 2 1

Wayland
An imprint of
Hachette Children's Group
Part of Hodder & Stoughton
Carmelite House
50 Victoria Embankment
London EC4Y 0DZ

An Hachette UK Company
www.hachette.co.uk
www.hachettechildrens.co.uk

Printed in China

Cover illustrations © Lee Hodges
Cover image © Historic England Publishing
images © Historic England Publishing: 1, 3tr, 3br, 5, 6, 7t, 8, 10, 13, 15, 19, 20, 21, 26, 27, 28, 29t
image © Tim Daw: 17b
illustrations by Kerry Hyndman: 5, 11, 12, 14, 15, 17, 18

Picture credits:
Corbis 23t; Dreamstime 7b, 9t, 23br, 24, 29b; Getty 31, 4; iStockPhoto 24t; Shutterstock 16, 25